Money
Talks

**Compiled by
Susan Teltser-Schwarz**

**Illustrated by
Thomas Sperling**

PETER PAUPER PRESS, INC.
WHITE PLAINS • NEW YORK

$$

A COMPILATION OF QUOTATIONS

AND PROVERBS, BOTH WITTY AND

WISE, ON THE SUBJECT OF

MONEY, FILTHY LUCRE, AND JUST

PLAIN CASH.

$$

MONEY TALKS

That money talks
I'll not deny,
I heard it once:
It said, "Goodbye."

Richard Armour

Money is better than poverty, if only for financial reasons.

Woody Allen

Money is like muck, not good except it be spread.

Francis Bacon

Money brings some happiness. But after a certain point it just brings more money.

Neil Simon

Money can't buy friends but you can get a better class of enemy.

Spike Milligan

When I was young I thought that money was the most important thing in life; now that I am old I know that it is.

OSCAR WILDE

The love of money is the root of all evil.

I TIMOTHY 6:10

Money is the root of all good.

AYN RAND

The two most beautiful words in the English language are "Cheque Enclosed".

DOROTHY PARKER

Money: A good thing to have. It frees you from doing things you dislike. Since I dislike doing nearly everything, money is handy.

GROUCHO MARX

Money is like a sixth sense—and you can't make use of the other five without it.

SOMERSET MAUGHAM

It is physically impossible for a well-educated, intellectual, or brave man to make money the chief object of his thoughts.

JOHN RUSKIN

There are only two families in the world, my old grandmother used to say, the *Haves* and the *Have-nots.*

MIGUEL DE CERVANTES

Money won't buy happiness, but it will pay the salaries of a large research staff to study the problem.

BILL VAUGHAN

There is only one thing for a man to do who is married to a woman who enjoys spending money, and that is to enjoy earning it.

EDGAR WATSON HOWE

I've been rich and I've been poor. Believe me, honey, rich is better.

SOPHIE TUCKER

You must spend money, if you wish to make money.

LATIN PROVERB

Money often costs too much.

RALPH WALDO EMERSON

Not many Americans have been around the world but their money sure has.

WALTER SLEZAK

If a man saves $15 a week and invests in good common stocks and allows the dividends and rights to accumulate, at the end of twenty years he will have at least $80,000. He will have an income from investments of around $400 a month. He will be rich. And because income can do that, I am firm in my belief that anyone not only can be rich but ought to be rich.

JOHN J. RASKOB (1928)

Money is applause.

JACQUELINE SUSANN

One by one the solid scholars
Get the degrees, the jobs, the dollars.
W. D. SNODGRASS

Some folks seem to get the idea that they're
worth a lot of money just because they
have it.
SETH PARKER

Money, it turned out, was exactly like sex, you
thought of nothing else if you didn't have it
and thought of other things if you did.
JAMES BALDWIN

Money talks.
FRENCH PROVERB

If you can count your money, you don't have a
billion dollars.
J. PAUL GETTY

Money makes the man.
ARISTODEMUS

I do everything for a reason . . . Most of the time the reason is money.

SUZY PARKER

To obtain a livelihood from a man is often like obtaining honey from a bee: it is accompanied by a sting.

NAFTALI OF ROPSHITZ

"How can I show my appreciation?" said a woman client to Clarence Darrow, after he had won her legal case. "My dear madam," said the great lawyer, "ever since the Phoenicians invented money there has been only one answer to that question."

He who has money has in his pocket those who have none.

LEO N. TOLSTOY

Put not your trust in money, but put your money in trust.

OLIVER WENDELL HOLMES

The real wealth of a nation resides in its farms and factories and the people who man them. A dynamic economy producing goods competitively priced in world markets will maintain the strength of the dollar.

JOHN F. KENNEDY

You can never be too thin or too rich.

MRS. WILLIAM (BABE) PALEY, THE DUCHESS OF WINDSOR, AND OTHERS

Wealth is not without its advantages and the case to the contrary, although it has often been made, has never proved widely persuasive.

JOHN KENNETH GALBRAITH

October. This is one of the peculiarly dangerous months to speculate in stocks in. The others are July, January, September, April, November, May, March, June, December, August, and February.

MARK TWAIN

Penny wise, pound foolish.

BURTON

Money doesn't always bring happiness. People with ten million dollars are no happier than people with nine million dollars.

HOBART BROWN

We women don't care too much about getting our pictures on money as long as we can get our hands on it.

IVY BAKER PRIEST

A fool and his money are soon parted.

GEORGE BUCHANAN

Never invest your money in anything that eats or needs repairing.

BILLY ROSE

Creditors have better memories than debtors.

BENJAMIN FRANKLIN

Take care of the pence, and the pounds will take care of themselves.

WILLIAM LOWNDES

I like to walk about amidst the beautiful things that adorn the world; but private wealth I should decline, or any sort of personal possessions, because they would take away my liberty.

GEORGE SANTAYANA

I was born into it and there was nothing I could do about it. It was there, like air or food or any other element . . . The only question with wealth is what you do with it.

JOHN D. ROCKEFELLER, JR.

For money has a power above
The stars and fate, to manage love.

SAMUEL BUTLER

Just as riches are an impediment to virtue in the wicked, so in the good they are an aid of virtue.

ST. AMBROSE

The purse strings tie us to our kind.

WALTER BAGEHOT

About money, former Mayor Edward Kelly of Chicago expressed the universal feeling more pithily and brightly than all the Latin epigrams and Persian wisecracks to be found in the books of quotations. He said: "Money is a strange commodity and a baffling subject. Time and again it has been proved a non-essential to happiness. It doesn't buy life, affect law, assure the respect of other men or win a place for its possessor in thinking society. I am referring, of course, to Confederate money."

GILBERT SELDES

If you would know the value of money, go and try to borrow some.

BENJAMIN FRANKLIN

You pays your money and you takes your choice.

PUNCH

As a general rule, nobody has money who ought to have it.

BENJAMIN DISRAELI

It is better to have a permanent income than to be fascinating.

OSCAR WILDE

Money is worth nothing to the man who has more than enough.

GEORGE BERNARD SHAW

If money go before, all ways do lie open.

WILLIAM SHAKESPEARE

Money is what you'd get on beautifully without if only other people weren't so crazy about it.

MARGARET CASE HARRIMAN

The money-getter is never tired.

CHINESE PROVERB

The rich are different from you and me because they have more credit.

JOHN LEONARD

I'd like to live like a poor man with lots of money.

PABLO PICASSO

Riches are not forbidden, but the pride of them is.

ST. JOHN CHRYSOSTOM

Money is like manure. If you spread it around it does a lot of good, but if you pile it up in one place it stinks like hell.

CLINT MURCHISON

A patch on your coat, and money in your pocket, is better and more creditable, than a writ on your back, and no money to take it off.

BENJAMIN FRANKLIN

Money itself isn't the primary factor in what one does. A person does things for the sake of accomplishing something. Money generally follows.

COLONEL HENRY CROWN

He that trusteth in his riches shall fall.

PROVERBS 11:28

One has a duty to make money, but only by honorable means. It is also one's duty to save money and increase it by diligence and thrift.

CICERO

Gold is gold though it be in a rogue's purse.

DANISH PROVERB

Let us all be happy and live within our means, even if we have to borrow the money to do it with.

CHARLES FARRAR BROWNE ("ARTEMUS WARD")

A heavy purse makes a light heart.

PROVERB

Money never comes out of season.

FRENCH PROVERB

The next hundred dollars he gets will not be worth more than ten that he used to get.

HENRY DAVID THOREAU

Money may be the husk of many things, but not the kernel. It brings you food, but not appetite; medicine, but not health; acquaintances, but not friends; servants, but not loyalty; days of joy, but not peace or happiness.

HENRIK IBSEN

Money buys everything, except morality and citizens.

JEAN-JACQUES ROUSSEAU

Go into the street, and give one man a lecture on morality, and another a shilling, and see which will respect you the most.

SAMUEL JOHNSON

It seems to be a law of American life that whatever enriches us anywhere except in the wallet inevitably becomes uneconomic.

RUSSELL BAKER

A rich man told me recently that a liberal is a man who tells other people what to do with their money.

LEROI JONES

All things that are exchanged must be somehow compared. It is for this end that money has been introduced, and it becomes in a sense an intermediate; for it measures all things.

ARISTOTLE

If one-half of a man's schemes turned out according to his preliminary figures, he would have nothing to do but spend his money.

BOB EDWARDS

I don't like money, actually, but it quiets my nerves.

JOE LOUIS

There is nothing so habit-forming as money.

DON MARQUIS

It's a kind of spiritual snobbery that makes people think they can be happy without money.

ALBERT CAMUS

Many a man would have been worse if his estate had been better.

BENJAMIN FRANKLIN

As wealth is power, so all power will infallibly draw wealth to itself by some means or other.

EDMUND BURKE

Just as war is waged with the blood of others, fortunes are made with other people's money.

ANDRÉ SUARÈS

The lawful basis of wealth is, that a man who works should be paid the fair value of his work, and that if he does not choose to spend it today, he should have free leave to keep it, and spend it tomorrow.

JOHN RUSKIN

Inherited wealth is a big handicap to happiness. It is as certain death to ambition as cocaine is to morality.

W. K. VANDERBILT

It is a socialist idea that making profits is a vice; I consider that the real vice is making losses.

WINSTON CHURCHILL

Money is not so important as a pat on the head.

LORD SNOW

The universal regard for money is the one hopeful fact in our civilization.

GEORGE BERNARD SHAW

He who multiplies Riches multiplies Cares.

BENJAMIN FRANKLIN

Money has no legs, but it runs.

ITALIAN PROVERB

The only people who claim that money is not important are people who have enough money so that they are relieved of the ugly burden of thinking about it.

JOYCE CAROL OATES

Money entails duties. How shall we get the money and forget the duties? Voilà the great problem!

EDWARD CARPENTER

It cuts off from life, from vitality, from the alive sun and the alive earth, as *nothing* can. Nothing, not even the most fanatical dogmas of an iron-bound religion, can insulate us from the inrush of life and inspiration, as money can.

D. H. LAWRENCE

The bread that you store up belongs to the hungry; the cloak that lies in your chest belongs to the naked; and the gold that you have hidden in the ground belongs to the poor.

ST. BASIL

To sum it up, money totals!

SUSAN TELTSER-SCHWARZ

Money is a terrible master but an excellent servant.

P. T. BARNUM

There are plenty of good five-cent cigars in the country. The trouble is they cost a quarter. What the country really needs is a good five-cent nickel.

FRANKLIN PIERCE ADAMS ("F.P.A.")

There are two times in a man's life when he should not speculate: when he can't afford it, and when he can.

MARK TWAIN

Money is sharper than a sword.

AFRICAN PROVERB

A purse without money is only a piece of leather.

JEWISH PROVERB

Pay what you owe, and you'll know what is your own.

BENJAMIN FRANKLIN

It is a good thing to be rich, and a good thing to be strong, but it is a better thing to be beloved of many friends.

EURIPIDES

Priorities are reflected in the things we spend money on. Far from being a dry accounting of bookkeepers, a nation's budget is full of moral implications; it tells what a society cares about and what it does not care about; it tells what its values are.

J. W. FULBRIGHT

Poverty is slavery.

AFRICAN PROVERB

The entire essence of America is the hope to first make money—then make money with money—then make lots of money with lots of money.

PAUL ERDMAN

Taking it all in all, I find it is more trouble to watch after money than to get it.

MONTAIGNE

Even the wisest among men welcome people who bring money more than those who take it away.

G. C. LICHTENBERG

Wealth: Any income that is at least $100 more a year than the income of one's wife's sister's husband.

H. L. MENCKEN

Almost any man knows how to earn money, but not one in a million knows how to spend it.

HENRY DAVID THOREAU

It takes a great deal of boldness mixed with a vast amount of caution, to acquire a great fortune; but then it takes ten times as much wit to keep it after you have got it as it took to make it.

MAYER A. ROTHSCHILD

Credit is a system whereby a person who can't pay gets another person who can't pay to guarantee that he can pay.

CHARLES DICKENS

I'm opposed to millionaires, but it would be dangerous to offer me the position.

MARK TWAIN

To suppose, as we all suppose, that we could be rich and not behave as the rich behave, is like supposing that we could drink all day and stay sober.

LOGAN PEARSALL SMITH

I have enough money to get by. I'm not independently wealthy, just independently lazy, I suppose.

MONTGOMERY CLIFT

The art of government consists in taking as much money as possible from one class of citizens to give it to the other.

VOLTAIRE

All things obey money.

CHAUCER

Wealth is the means, and people are the ends. All our material riches will avail us little if we do not use them to expand the opportunities of our people.

JOHN F. KENNEDY

Of evils current upon earth, the worst is money. It is money that sacks cities, and drives men forth from hearth and home; warps and seduces native innocence, and breeds a habit of dishonesty.

SOPHOCLES

It is a common observation that any fool can get money; but they are not wise that think so.

C. C. COLTON

Never in the history of human credit has so much been owed.

MARGARET THATCHER

Let us turn bottoms up and drink to the health of those who advocate sharing the wealth. A dandy good scheme, a boon to the nation, and I'm tooth and nail for it—with this reservation:

That I be allowed to pick a "sharee" like Mellon or Morgan or Ford or John D. But if I'm expected to cast in my lot, and share with a guy who has less than I've got, the whole scheme is the bunkum—there's nothing in it, so put in the record that I'm dead agin' it.

ASHTON HILL

Comedian Richard Pryor, critically burned in an accident, told Johnny Carson that when you're seriously ill, money isn't important. He said: "All I could think of was to call on God. I didn't call the Bank of America once."

In investing money the amount of interest you want should depend on whether you want to eat well or sleep well.

J. K. MORLEY

Money speaks sense in a language all nations understand.

APHRA BEHN

Money has wings.

FRENCH PROVERB

Money's a good plaster, and a wad of hundred-franc notes can be spread over quite a bruise.

P. C. WREN

Blessed is the man who has both mind and money, for he employs the latter well.

MENANDER

If you would know what the Lord God thinks of money, you have only to look at those to whom he gives it.

MAURICE BARING

Make all you can, save all you can, give all you can.

JOHN WESLEY

Money makes its own mores!

SUSAN TELTSER-SCHWARZ

Everyone gives himself credit for more brains than he has and less money.

ITALIAN PROVERB

Can anybody remember when the times were not hard and money not scarce?

RALPH WALDO EMERSON

Money is the soul of business.

GERMAN PROVERB

The fuel that keeps the new people moving faster than the speed of worry is money.

WILFRID SHEED

Anybody can make a fortune. It takes genius to hold on to one.

JAY GOULD (ATTRIBUTED)

A man who has money may be anxious, depressed, frustrated and unhappy, but one thing he's not—and that's broke.

BRENDAN FRANCIS

No man divulges his revenue, or at least
which way it comes in; but everyone publishes
his acquisitions.

MONTAIGNE

Nothing is sadder than the consequences of
having worldly standards without worldly
means.

VAN WYCK BROOKS

Money alone sets all the world in motion.

PUBLILIUS SYRUS

The world is his, who has money to go
over it.

RALPH WALDO EMERSON

The money power preys upon the Nation in
times of peace and conspires against it in
times of adversity. It is more despotic than
monarchy, more insolent than autocracy,
more selfish than bureaucracy. It denounces,
as public enemies, all who question its
methods, or throw light upon its crimes.

WILLIAM JENNINGS BRYAN

My power is as great as is the power of money. The qualities of money are my—the possessor's—qualities and potentialities. What I *am* and *can do,* therefore, is by no means determined by my individuality. I *am* ugly, but I can buy the *most beautiful* woman. So I am not *ugly,* for the effect of *ugliness,* its repulsive power, is eliminated by money.

KARL MARX

Riches prick us with a thousand troubles in getting them, as many cares in preserving them, and with yet more anxieties in spending them, and with grief in losing them.

J. P. CAMUS

A man who has a million dollars is as well off as if he were rich.

JOHN JACOB ASTOR III *(ATTRIBUTED)*

The production of wealth is not the work of any one man, and the acquisition of great fortunes is not possible without the cooperation of multitudes of men.

PETER COOPER

Money is not required to buy one necessity of the soul.

HENRY DAVID THOREAU

I am far from underestimating the importance of dividends; but I rank dividends below human character.

THEODORE ROOSEVELT

As soon as any art is pursued with a view to money, then farewell, in ninety-nine cases out of a hundred, all hope of genuine good work.

SAMUEL BUTLER

The great monopoly in this country is the money monopoly. So long as it exists, our old variety of freedom and individual energy of development are out of the question.

WOODROW WILSON

A rich man is nothing but a poor man with money.

W. C. FIELDS

I'm tired of Love, I'm still more tired of
   Rhyme,
But money gives me pleasure all the time.
                              HILAIRE BELLOC

There is no stronger craving in the world than
that of the rich for titles, except that of the
titled for riches.
                              HESKETH PEARSON

The art of making yourself rich, in the
ordinary mercantile economic sense, is therefore equally and necessarily the art of keeping
your neighbour poor.
                              JOHN RUSKIN

No one would remember the Good Samaritan
if he only had good intentions. He had money
as well.
                              MARGARET THATCHER

The poor have little,—beggars none;
The rich too much—enough not one.
                              BENJAMIN FRANKLIN

I've realized, after fourteen months in this country, the value of money, whether it is clean or dirty.

NGUYEN CAO KY

We reckon hours and minutes to be dollars and cents.

THOMAS CHANDLER HALIBURTON ("SAM SLICK")

One handful of money is stronger than two handfuls of truth.

DANISH PROVERB

If a man is wise, he gets rich, and if he gets rich, he gets foolish, or his wife does.

FINLEY PETER DUNNE

It's our own money and we're free to spend it any way we please. It's part of this campaign business. If you have money, you spend it to win. And the more you can afford, the more you'll spend. It's something that is not regulated. Therefore, it's not unethical.

ROSE KENNEDY

If one-half of a man's schemes turned out according to his preliminary figures, he would have nothing to do but spend his money.

BOB EDWARDS

A great estate is not gotten in a few hours.

FRENCH PROVERB

The happiest time in any man's life is when he is in red-hot pursuit of a dollar with a reasonable prospect of overtaking it.

HENRY WHEELER SHAW ("JOSH BILLINGS")

He who has no money in his purse should have honey on his tongue.

FRENCH PROVERB

The price we have to pay for money is paid in liberty.

ROBERT LOUIS STEVENSON

Money draws money.

YIDDISH PROVERB

Wealth maketh many friends; but the poor is separated from his neighbours.

BIBLICAL PROVERB

To be clever enough to get a great deal of money, one must be stupid enough to want it.

G. K. CHESTERTON

If you have money, take a seat; if not, stand on your feet.

GERMAN PROVERB

Money is the most important thing in the world.

GEORGE BERNARD SHAW

In God we trust; all others must pay cash.

AMERICAN SAYING

The money paid, the work delayed.

SPANISH PROVERB

Wealth is the product of man's capacity to think.

AYN RAND

As quickly as you start spending federal money in large amounts, it looks like free money.

DWIGHT D. EISENHOWER

He that is of the opinion Money will do every Thing may well be suspected of doing every Thing for Money.

BENJAMIN FRANKLIN

A small coin before the eyes will hide the biggest mountain.

NACHMAN OF BRATZLAV

Everything else can satisfy only *one* wish, *one* need; ... Money alone is absolutely good, because it is not only a concrete satisfaction of one need in particular; it is an abstract satisfaction of all.

ARTHUR SCHOPENHAUER

The art of getting rich consists not in industry, much less in saving, but in a better order, in timeliness, in being at the right spot.

RALPH WALDO EMERSON

It's no use filling your pocket full of money if you've got a hole in the corner.

GEORGE ELIOT

Money is the common denominator of ambition.

SUSAN TELTSER-SCHWARZ

The first of all English games is making money.

JOHN RUSKIN

Plenty of people despise money, but few know how to give it away.

LA ROCHEFOUCAULD

Getting money is like digging with a needle; spending it is like water soaking into sand.

JAPANESE PROVERB

All those men have their price.

SIR ROBERT WALPOLE
(referring to certain members of Parliament)

Money begets money.

ITALIAN PROVERB

Nothing is more fallacious than wealth. Today it is for thee, tomorrow it is against thee. It arms the eyes of the envious everywhere. It is a hostile comrade, a domestic enemy.

ST. JOHN CHRYSOSTOM

Money is always on the brain so long as there is a brain in reasonable order.

SAMUEL BUTLER

The rich are always complaining.

AFRICAN PROVERB

When a man says money can do anything, that settles it: he hasn't any.

E. W. HOWE

Money is the only Monarch.

THOMAS FULLER

No mountain is so high that an ass loaded with gold cannot climb it.

SPANISH PROVERB

The dollars aren't important—once you have them.

JOHNNY MILLER

It costs a lot of money to die comfortably.

SAMUEL BUTLER

Get money first; virtue comes afterward.

HORACE

Ready money is Aladdin's lamp.

LORD BYRON

Money is flat and meant to be piled up.

SCOTTISH PROVERB

Money swore an oath that nobody that did not love it should ever have it.

IRISH PROVERB

There is no fortress so strong that money cannot take it.

CICERO

Wealth consists not in having great possessions but in having few wants.

EPICURUS

When it is a question of money, everybody is of the same religion.

VOLTAIRE

He that makes money before he gets wit,
Will be but a short while the master of it.

THOMAS FULLER

But the jingling of the guinea helps the hurt that Honour feels.

ALFRED, LORD TENNYSON

When wealth is centralized the people are dispersed; when wealth is distributed the people are brought together.

CONFUCIUS

He who loves money must labor.

AFRICAN PROVERB

Money wasn't that important. Money doesn't help you sleep. Money doesn't help your mother be well, money doesn't make your brother stay interested in his studies, money don't help an argument when nobody knows what they're arguing about. Money don't help nothing. Money is only good when you've got something else to do with it. A man can lose everything, family, all your dreams, and still have a pocketful of money.

GEORGE FOREMAN

A gentleman of our days is one who has money enough to do what every fool would do if he could afford it: that is, consume without producing.

GEORGE BERNARD SHAW

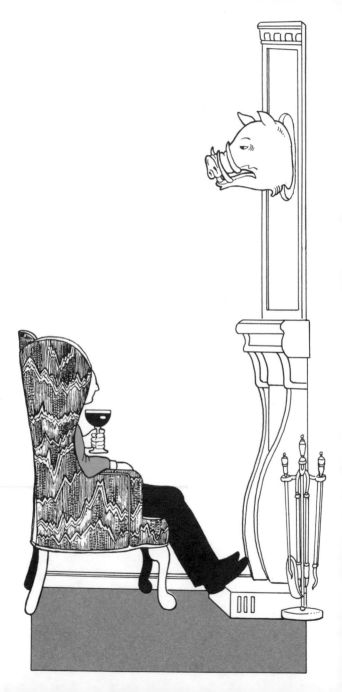

Money alone can't bring you happiness, but money alone has not brought me unhappiness ... I won't say my previous husbands thought only of my money, but it had a certain fascination for them.

BARBARA HUTTON

Spare no expense to make everything as economical as possible.

SAM GOLDWYN

Money is like the reputation for ability—more easily made than kept.

SAMUEL BUTLER

Every little penny eventually adds up to a large sum.

TALMUD

Money is a guarantee that we may have what we want in the future. Though we need nothing at the moment it insures the possibility of satisfying a new desire when it arises.

ARISTOTLE

Disgusted at being considered a genius by every person when he at all times attempted to make himself appear perfectly normal, Rachmaninoff came up with the retort courteous when a stagestruck listener gurgled, "What ever inspired you to compose such a wonderfully marvelous piece as your C-Sharp Minor Prelude?"

The master made a deep bow and, with a perfectly composed face, replied, "Because, madam, I needed the dough."

We often buy money very much too dear.
WILLIAM MAKEPEACE THACKERAY

Our problem is not what the dollar is worth at home or abroad—it's how to get hold of it, whatever it's worth.
WILL ROGERS

I have always thought it was the first task of an economist to provide himself with a certain minimum of money. The fact I was able to do that without too much mental strain has never bothered me.
JOHN KENNETH GALBRAITH

A full purse never lacks friends.

PROVERB

Well, fancy giving money to the Government!
  Might as well have put it down the drain.
Fancy giving money to the Government!
  Nobody will see the stuff again.
Well, they've no idea what money's for—
  Ten to one they'll start another war.
I've heard a lot of silly things, but, Lor'!
  Fancy giving money to the Government!

SIR ALAN PATRICK HERBERT

The almighty dollar, that great object of universal devotion throughout our land.

WASHINGTON IRVING

God made bees, and bees made honey,
God made man, and man made money.

AUTHOR UNIDENTIFIED

We all know how the size of sums of money appears to vary in a remarkable way according as they are being paid in or paid out.

JULIAN HUXLEY

The safest way to double your money is to fold it over once and put it in your pocket.

KIN HUBBARD

No man will take counsel, but every man will take money: therefore money is better than counsel.

JONATHAN SWIFT

One man's pay increase is another man's price increase.

HAROLD WILSON

Money you know will hide many faults.

MIGUEL DE CERVANTES

Wealth is a power usurped by the few, to compel the many to labor for their benefit.

P. B. SHELLEY

A good cause and a good tongue: and yet money must carry it.

THOMAS FULLER

Annual income twenty pounds, annual expenditure nineteen pounds six, result happiness. Annual income twenty pounds, annual expenditure twenty pounds ought and six, result misery.

CHARLES DICKENS

There is nothing earthly that lasts so well, on the whole, as money. A man's learning dies with him; even his virtues fade out of remembrance; but the dividends on the stocks he bequeaths to his children live and keep his memory green.

OLIVER WENDELL HOLMES, SR.

A wealthy man will always have followers.

AFRICAN PROVERB

One cannot count on riches.

AFRICAN PROVERB

I cannot understand why men should be so eager after money. Wealth is simply a superfluity of what we don't need.

ABRAHAM LINCOLN

There are few ways in which a man can be more innocently employed than in getting money.

SAMUEL JOHNSON

Money, n. A blessing that is of no advantage to us excepting when we part with it.

AMBROSE BIERCE

It saves a lot of trouble if, instead of having to earn money and save it, you can just go and borrow it.

WINSTON CHURCHILL

Money is indeed the most important thing in the world; and all sound and successful personal and national morality should have this fact for its basis.

GEORGE BERNARD SHAW

Nothing is more admirable than the fortitude with which millionaires tolerate the disadvantages of their wealth.

REX STOUT

Superfluous wealth can buy superfluities
only.

HENRY DAVID THOREAU

    Learn to give
Money to colleges while you live.
Don't be silly and think you'll try
To bother the colleges, when you die,
With codicil this, and codicil that,
That knowledge may starve while Law grows
    fat;
For there never was pitcher that wouldn't
    spill,
And there's always a flaw in a donkey's will.

OLIVER WENDELL HOLMES

A man is usually more careful of his money
than he is of his principles.

EDGAR WATSON HOWE

Money is a new form of slavery, and distin-
guishable from the old simply by the fact that
it is impersonal—that there is no human
relation between master and slave.

LEO N. TOLSTOY

Stand not too near the rich man lest he destroy thee—and not too far away lest he forget thee.

ANEURIN BEVAN

Money is, with propriety, considered as the vital principle of the body politic; as that which sustains its life and motion, and enables it to perform its most essential functions. A complete power, therefore, to procure a regular and adequate supply of it, as far as the resources of the community will permit, may be regarded as an indispensable ingredient in every constitution. From a deficiency in this particular, one of two evils must ensue; either the people must be subjected to continual plunder, as a substitute for a more eligible mode of supplying the public wants, or the government must sink into a fatal atrophy, and, in a short course of time, perish.

ALEXANDER HAMILTON

With the great part of rich people, the chief employment of riches consists in the parade of riches.

ADAM SMITH

Remember that time is money.

BENJAMIN FRANKLIN

How pleasant it is to have money, heigh ho;
How pleasant it is to have money.

ARTHUR HUGH CLOUGH

The advantage of keeping family accounts is
clear. If you do not keep them you are
uneasily aware of the fact that you are
spending more than you are earning. If you
do keep them, you *know* it.

ROBERT BENCHLEY

Money is a soap that removes the worst
stains.

JEWISH PROVERB

The difference between a little money and no
money at all is enormous—and can shatter
the world. And the difference between a little
money and an enormous amount of money is
very slight—and that, also, can shatter the
world.

THORNTON WILDER

The only thing I like about rich people is their money.

LADY ASTOR

There is no society, however free and democratic, where wealth will not create an aristocracy.

BULWER

The only thing that hurts more than paying an income tax is not having to pay an income tax.

THOMAS R. DEWAR

The covetous man never has money; the prodigal will have none shortly.

BEN JONSON

A drunkard would not give money to sober people. He said they would only eat it, and buy clothes and send their children to school with it.

SAMUEL BUTLER

The rich man and his daughter are soon parted.

FRANK MCKINNEY HUBBARD

There are men who gain from their wealth only the fear of losing it.

ANTOINE RIVAROLI

Without money, honor is a malady.

RACINE

Poor people always lean forward when they speak because they want people to listen to them. Rich people can sit back.

MICHAEL CAINE

In the progress of time, and through our own base carelessness and ignorance, we have permitted the money-industry, by virtue of its business, to gradually attain a political and economic influence so powerful that it has actually undermined the authority of the State and usurped the power of Democratic government.

VINCENT C. VICKERS

I would rather have a man that wants money,
than money that wants a man.

THEMISTOCLES
*(preferring that an honest man, rather than a rich
man, woo his daughter)*

There are few sorrows, however poignant, in
which a good income is of no avail.

LOGAN PEARSALL SMITH

Riches do not gain hearty respect: they only
procure external attention.

SAMUEL JOHNSON

Money is the best bait to fish for man with.

THOMAS FULLER

The makers of fortunes have a second love of
money as a creation of their own, resembling
the affection of authors for their own poems,
or of parents for their children, besides that
natural love of it for the sake of use and
profit.

PLATO

If a man runs after money, he's money-mad; if he keeps it, he's a capitalist; if he spends it, he's a playboy; if he doesn't get it, he's a ne'er-do-well; if he doesn't try to get it, he lacks ambition. If he gets it without working for it, he's a parasite; and if he accumulates it after a lifetime of hard work, people call him a fool who never got anything out of life.

VIC OLIVER

Wealth *per se* I never too much valued, and my acquaintance with its possessors has by no means increased my veneration for it.

FRANCES BURNEY

Very few men acquire wealth in such a manner as to receive pleasure from it.

HENRY WARD BEECHER

But it is pretty to see what money will do.

SAMUEL PEPYS

The money you refuse will never do you any good.

ITALIAN PROVERB

The man who thinks that anything can be accomplished by money is likely to do anything for money.

JEWISH SAYING

A man's wealth may be superior to him.

AFRICAN PROVERB

The power which money gives is that of brute force; it is the power of the bludgeon and the bayonet.

WILLIAM COBBETT

For what is worth in anything
But so much money as 'twill bring?

SAMUEL BUTLER

The rich get richer and the poor get poorer.

ANDREW CARNEGIE

Better a steady dime than a rare dollar.

JEWISH SAYING

Surplus wealth is a sacred trust which its possessor is bound to administer in his lifetime for the good of the community.

ANDREW CARNEGIE

If you make money your god, it will plague you like the devil.

HENRY FIELDING

If rich people could hire other people to die for them, the poor could make a wonderful living.

YIDDISH PROVERB

Not having to worry about money is almost like not having to worry about dying.

MARIO PUZO

Shrouds have no pockets.

JEWISH SAYING

It is better to live rich than to die rich.

SAMUEL JOHNSON

Money Glossary; To Coin a Phrase

Nouns
Bread *(slang)*—sustenance, livelihood, as in *to earn one's bread*

Cash—currency

Dough *(slang)*—money

Mad money *(slang)*—small sum kept in reserve, usually by a woman, for an emergency

Means—available resources, especially money

Moola or moolah *(slang)*—money

Scratch *(slang)*—cash

Spending money—money for small personal expenses

Adjectives
Munificent—extremely liberal, very generous

Niggardly—reluctant to give or spend, miserly

Parsimonious—tight, stingy

Penny-pinching—stingy, niggardly

Prodigal—spending lavishly, extravagant, wasteful

Money Types
Miser—one who saves and hoards money

Money bags *(slang)*—a wealthy person

Skinflint *(slang)*—miser

Spendthrift—a person who spends money extravagantly or wastefully

Tightwad *(slang)*—a stingy person

Green stuff *(slang)*—paper money (which is green in some countries)